Break the Binge Spending: A Complete Guide on Frugal Living

How to Control Spending and Regain Financial Freedom

By: Stephen Harris

9781634286893

I0510903

PUBLISHERS NOTES

Disclaimer – Speedy Publishing LLC

Speedy Publishing LLC

40 E Main Street, Newark, Delaware, 19711

Contact Us: 1-888-248-4521

Website: http://www.speedypublishing.co

REPRINTED Paperback Edition: ISBN: 9781634286893

Manufactured in the United States of America

DEDICATION

I dedicate this book to my late father, Alfred. He raised me well and taught me how to live simply and happily.

TABLE OF CONTENTS

Publishers Notes.. 2

Dedication 3

Table of Contents.. 4

Chapter 1- Spending and Start Living Within your Means 5

Chapter 2- Other Options to Stop Binge Spending 10

Chapter 3- Stop Binge Spending and Start Earning More 15

Chapter 4- Binge Spending with Your Credit Card is a Sin 19

Chapter 5- Signs and Symptoms that you're a Binge Spender ...21

Chapter 6- Binge Spending: Society Dictates.......................................31

Chapter 7- Binge Spending: Assess your Financial Status 38

Chapter 8- Binge Spending: Financial Priorities 42

Chapter 9- Binge Spending vs. Habitual Saving................................48

Chapter 10- Tips and Summary on How to do Away Binge
Spending 58

About The Author...62

CHAPTER 1- SPENDING AND START LIVING WITHIN YOUR MEANS

If you really want to discover the art of living happily with less than you've ever imagined before, living within your means is the first thing that you should know and be aware of. It is true that living with your means merely involves setting up of your specific goals since setting up your goals will greatly influence your budget setting.

When it comes to budget, it is very normal that it is associated with saving and spending activities. In addition to this, living within your means also involves spending your money wisely. It is very important that you know the basics of living within your means to make sure that you will not find hard time and difficulty in saving and spending the money that you have.

Beyond the Diet with Healthy Diet Recipes

In order for you to be familiar with the basics of living within your means, here are some of the salient tips on how to live within your means. By simply following these tips, you can be sure that you will live a happy life that you dreamed of.

The Salient Tips on How to Live Within your Means

Living within your means involves important tips that will greatly help you to save and spend the money that you have. It is very imperative that you are aware about the proper way to live within your means in order to attain a happy life that you dreamed of.

• Maintaining your Balanced Budget

In order to completely maintain a balanced budget, the first thing that you need to do is to create your own list of your basic needs like clothing, utilities and groceries. These things are also considered as essentials since these are the things that you cannot live without. Moreover, you are also required to create your budget by simply examining your expenditures and income. By doing this, you can easily determine how much money you will spend and save.

• Estimate your Earnings

Estimating your monthly income is highly recommended. If you have regular job, it would be easier for you to estimate your monthly budget however if you have part time job, it is very normal that you will find difficulty in estimating and budgeting your budget. In estimating your budget, you need to make sure that you separate the amount of money that is intended for taxes.

• Record your Expenditures

In order for you to easily determine your expenditures, you need to record the items that you bought and the total amount of money that you spend. By doing this, you can easily track the amount of money that you spend in buying those essential items and non-essential things.

• Compare your expenditures to your income

If you notice that your expenditures and income are just equal, it simply means that you are not saving any amount of money. However, if your expenditures are higher than your monthly income, it is a big problem.

• Evaluate the Expenditures

By simply evaluating your expenditures, you will easily determine where your budget is going. It is very important to categorize your essentials like eating out. When you already created your own category, this is the best time for you to sum up all your purchases in every category of your expenditures.

Distinguish Between Wants and Needs

When it comes in living within your means, it is very important that you have a clear and better understanding about the difference between needs and wants. If you are aware about the difference between the two, you can be sure that you can keep out of unwanted debt.

Before you purchase anything, it is very imperative to ask yourself if you truly need it. If you don't need such thing, think again before buying. In the present year, most people are getting confused about the real difference of needs and wants.

In order for you to completely live a happy life that you dreamed of, understanding the difference between needs and wants is highly recommended. Here, you will know the accurate difference of needs and wants.

The Real Difference between Needs and Wants

Today, most people don't know the real difference between needs and wants. If this is one of the problems that you are encountering, this is the right time for you to know the definite definition of needs and wants. Needs can be defined as something that is extremely necessary for a certain individual to survive.

When your needs is not completely meet, you will have a great chance to experience illnesses and diseases and at the same time you cannot work properly. Needs are being categorized into 2 groups, the first one is the physical or objective needs.

Two Groups of Need

Objective Needs- These needs are being met through tangible items or things that can be measured such as air, shelter, water and food.

Subjective Needs- These needs are the one that is associated with mental health like approval, security and self esteem.

A want can be defined as something that a certain individual desires. Moreover, wants differ from individual to another person like when some individuals want to buy their own car while there are also other persons who want to travel in different places in the world.

Every person has their own wants however as time goes by, wants can easily be changed and this serve as the contrast of needs. Moreover, needs and wants are considered as economic terminologies that you should know and be aware of. The most common examples of need includes clothing, health care, hygiene products, foods, shelter, family outings and vacations, college expenses and fees, child education and house expenses. The usual examples of wants include expensive car, expensive clothes and extra vacation. Now, that you completely know the difference of needs and wants, the first thing that you should consider is to know the proper way on how to separate needs and wants.

In connection with this, you also need to know the real significance of needs and wants in order for you to live within your means. When you completely determine the difference between needs and wants, it would be easier for you to attain a happy life that you never imagined before. Distinguishing between wants and needs are considered as one of the salient factors that will greatly help you to live within your means. This is the first step that you should take into consideration especially if you really desire to explore the real significance of living within your means.

CHAPTER 2- OTHER OPTIONS TO STOP BINGE SPENDING

In order for you to save a lot of money from your budget, buying secondhand items, appliances and gadgets can be a helpful choice. In the present year, most people are struggling from lack of budget and this is one of the reasons why they prefer to buy secondhand items, appliances and gadgets.

If you completely decided to purchase secondhand items, it is very important that you consider the money and budget that you have. If you can't afford to buy the latest version of gadgets and appliances, buying secondhand items is the ideal option that you should take into account.

However in buying secondhand items, there are also advantages and disadvantages that you should be aware of. In order for you to have a clear and better understanding on buying secondhand items, here are some of the advantages and disadvantages that you need to ponder on.

The Advantages and Disadvantages of Buying Secondhand Items

Buying secondhand items will greatly help you to save more money that you can make use in sustaining the basic needs of your family. For example, you are planning to buy a new set of television however your budget is not enough to purchase a new one then, you can consider buying secondhand appliances.

In this way, you can save more money that you can make use during emergency purposes. It is very imperative that you know the proper way to spend the money that you have and this is one of the significance of living within your means.

Advantages of Buying Secondhand Items

• Price

One of the big differences that you will encounter in buying secondhand items is the price. It is a fact that buying secondhand items are less expensive compared to new one.

• Depreciation

In terms of depreciation, you will not experience it with secondhand items. Depreciation usually occurs in latest item since they need to maintain the value of the item as time goes by. For example, a new car has the ability to lose 40 percent of their overall value during the first year of your purchase. However, when you buy secondhand car, you don't need to worry about the mental depreciation.

• Insurance Rates

When you buy a new car, the insurance rates of your car will completely affected however with used cars, the insurance rates are less expensive. In this way, you can save from the so called sticker shock.

• Choice

If you really desire to buy secondhand car, you don't need to worry since in the present year, there are a wide selection of option package, wheel design and model that you can opt from.

Disadvantages of Buying Secondhand Items

• Short Life Span

Since most of the secondhand items are already been used by other people, it is very normal that you will experience short life span of secondhand items.

• Poor Maintenance

There are also secondhand items that you will find hard time and difficulty with their maintenance level. This is one of the disadvantages that you will encounter when you decided to buy secondhand items.

• Lack of Quality

There are also secondhand items that are lacking in quality since they are already used by the original owner. However, in choosing for the best secondhand items, you need to opt the one that is made from high quality materials in order for you to make sure that you will obtain the elite secondhand items that can last for a long period of time.

If you really want to live within your means and experience the amazing benefits of living a frugal life, the first factor that you should take into account is to never pay retail. According to experts, it is very important that you know the importance of great benefits of never paying the retail price.

It is true that most today really love to shop new and latest trends of clothes however in order for you to live within your means, this factor is the ideal tip that you should bear in mind.

In order for you to have an apparent and superior understanding about never pay the retail price, here are some of the facts that you should consider that will greatly help you to live within your means.

When you hear the term "never pay retail", what is the first thing that comes into your mind? If one of your goals in life is to live a frugal life within your means, this is the perfect time that you fully understand this salient factor in living within your means.

Facts you should know about Never Pay Retail

• Shop Sales- If one of your hobbies is shop for the newest fashion trends of clothes and heel shoes, this is the best time for you to know the importance of shop sales. If you want to buy those clothes and shoes now, you need to think again since in just six weeks time those items will offer you with 50 percent discount. It simply means that you just need to patient and wait for the upcoming shop sales of the items that you desire to buy.

Beyond the Diet with Healthy Diet Recipes

• Make use of the Coupon Codes- If you are one of those individuals who usually purchase items online, it is very imperative that you make use of your online coupon code and service. Most of the online stores don't advertise their online deals that include 20 percent discount and free shipping.

• Use Coupons- It is true that coupons are considered as the easiest and incredible way to save on professional services, household products and groceries. By simply using these coupons, you can be sure that you can save a huge amount of your money that you can make use on other emergency purposes.

• Second-hand Shop Sales- Today most people are still confused about the importance of second-hand stores, consignment shops and garage sales. Buying second-hand items will also help you to save money. All you need to bear in mind; you can also find valuable used items at second-hand stores, consignment shops and garage sales.

Chapter 3- Stop Binge Spending and Start Earning More

If you want to gain extra income that will help you to obtain a happy life that you dreamed of. Creating your own garden at home can be a great help to sustain the basic needs of your family. Garden with vegetables is the perfecto option that you should plant in your garden at home since when the time comes that you can already harvest your crops, you can sell it in the market and convert it to money.

The profit that you will get in selling the vegetables from your garden will help you to support your basic needs. You can add your profits from your monthly income and rest assured that you will not find hard time and difficulty in sustaining your daily needs. Here, you will know and learn more about the significance of creating your own garden at home.

The Significance of Creating your own Garden at Home

It is true that vegetable garden at home is considered as one of the easiest ways to easily save money. Most people who already try to create their own garden at home are all fulfilled and happy with the great results of their vegetable garden at home. In order for you to be familiar in creating a vegetable garden at home, here is some of the significance of having vegetable garden.

• The first thing that you should bear in mind is to choose the vegetables that you will plant in your garden at home. It is very important that you opt those vegetables that you can easily sell in the market. One of the best vegetables to plant in your vegetable garden is tomato since according to studies, tomato has the ability to provide your family with 10 pounds fruits especially during their course season.

• When you decided to plant a vegetable garden at home, it will give you with delicious vegetables that you serve for your lunch and dinner with your family. In this way, you can save a lot of your money. Instead of purchasing vegetables in the market, you can just harvest in the comfort of your vegetable garden at home.

• It is also true that growing delicious vegetables can be a great fun and source of family bonding. It simply means, you can spend a lot of time with your children and enjoy some of the outdoor activities like planting vegetables. However, it is very important that you creatively plan your vegetable garden to come up with the best possible outcomes that you are expecting.

• The next thing that you should do is to properly pick the best spot to create your own vegetable garden at home. In choosing for the best spot, it is very imperative to consider the three important requirements that include good soil, a lot of water and full sun. In the recent year, most of the gardeners preferred that their vegetable garden is near to their home. In this way, it would be easier for you to harvest the vegetables from your garden.

• It is also important that you know the best way to easily design your own vegetable garden. Planning and designing the layout of the vegetable garden are divided with 2 basic approaches that include row cropping and intensive cropping.

• Fixing and testing your soil is also one of the important factors that you should consider in maintaining your vegetable garden.

Cut Down on Waste

If you are one of those persons who are struggling to completely live within your means, one of the great factors that you should take into account is to cut down on waste and expenses. According to researches, cutting down on waste is recognized as one of the salient factors that you should bear in mind to easily and quickly live within your means.

It is very imperative that you are aware about the things that you should cut down in order to obtain the best possible results that you are expecting. Here, you will know and learn more about some of the things that you need to cut down to save money.

Things that you should cut down to save Money

In order for you to attain a fugal life, one of the factors that you should take into consideration is to cut down on waste and expenses. It is true that most people has their own set of lifestyle however when it comes to saving money for the future, you are recommended to cut down on waste and expenses.

In this way, you can be sure that you will attain a frugal life that you dreamed of. According to some people, living a frugal life is not an easy task at all since it requires hard work, time, effort, passion and dedication to make sure that you will get the best outcomes that you are looking for. Here are some of the things that you should cut down to save money.

• shopping trips

• cellphone bills

• cable TV

• nail and hair salons

• gym memberships

In order for you to easily save money that you can make use on the future, all you need to do is to check your bills and at the same time cancel those services that you don't usually use. When you decided to cut down all your non-essentials expenses, you can be sure that you are truly ready to explore the real world of living frugally and living within your means.

CHAPTER 4- BINGE SPENDING WITH YOUR CREDIT CARD IS A SIN

To completely enjoy a happy life that you dreamed of, the first thing that you should consider is to get rid of your credit card debts.

Most people in the present year usually experience credit card debt and most of them are seeking for the effective ways on how to easily get rid of their credit card debts. If you are still paying your credit card debts, you will not completely enjoy your money.

Paying all your credit card debts will greatly affect the overall budget of your family. Since most people really want to know the best ways to get rid of your credit card debts, here are some of the tips that you should follow to easily and quickly get rid of your credit card debts.

According to researches, credit card debts are considered as one of the usual problems of most people in the present year. Most people are seeking out for the easiest ways on how to easily and quickly get rid of their credit card debts. In order for you to fully understand this kind of scenario, it is very imperative that you are aware about some of the salient tips on how to get rid of your credit card debts.

The Useful Tips to Easily Get Rid of your Credit Card Debts

• Avoid Using Credit Card-If you really want to easily get rid of unwanted credit card debts, the first thing that you should take into consideration is to avoid using your credit card. This is the only way that you can do to prevent the occurrence of the stigma of credit card debts.

• Conquer and Divide-When it comes in avoiding your credit card debts, you must be aware and familiar with various strategies that you can make use to quickly eliminate your unwanted debts. The common strategy is to divide the overall total of your credit card debts by 12 then the next thing that you should do is to pay off the amount every month.

• Do Hustle-In order to this, you need to have extra earning to make sure that you can easily pay your debt in just a short period of time. Apart from this, you can also pick part time job to gain additional income and at the same time you can be sure that you can quickly kill your credit card debts.

• Keep Paying off-It is very important that you continue to pay your credit card debts until you completely pay all your debts. By doing this, you can be sure that you will surely enjoy your money and start saving funds for the future.

CHAPTER 5- SIGNS AND SYMPTOMS THAT YOU'RE A BINGE SPENDER

There are chemical couriers called neurotransmitters that convey communication from your brain to throughout your body. When you're nervous, nervous, or feeling concerned (like when self-critical ideas begin sneaking in), you receive a flood of panic-inducing epinephrine that may feel like undiluted jet fuel.

When something occurs that makes you feel particularly great (like when you purchase something!), you receive a rush of unbelievably satisfying neurotransmitters known as serotonins that feels dandy.

You've gotten inebriated by your own conduct. The only thing that feels crucial is to be able to carry on spending-- because shopping for and getting fresh stuff makes you feel so great about yourself, about your life story, about everything! Just like the definition for addiction states, you've surrendered yourself to a behavior that's chronic, obsessive, and impairs your critical functioning.

Spending dependency is a symptom—or blinking warning light-- that there are deep-seated feelings you're attempting to prevent facing. Indulging yourself in buying helps dull those disquieting feelings—for a while.

Each time you attempt to stop the practice of compulsive spending, you discover you have to deal with the disturbing feelings "cold turkey," and the terror and fear that crops up is nearly unspeakable. Even though you might have called yourself you were going to truly conquer your spending, in an endeavor to feel better quickly, you go on still a different shopping binge.

What feelings may be so painfully terrible that they're capable of placing you on a spending path of self- annihilation? Perhaps you're afraid that you're not as magnetic or successful as you would like to be. Maybe your fearfulness stems from trusting that the true you aren't lovable.

Or perhaps you're afraid that the window dressing—the "outer" you--you've worked so hard to construct and have maintained so fastidiously will collapse, and that other people will then see what, in your brain, is behind that front: that you're a sham, a fake, a loser.

When you have spending addiction, what you're really trying to "purchase" is to be liked and looked up to by other people and to not feel devoured by self-doubt and self- disappointment.

It doesn't matter how much income you have, how successful you are, or what prestige you bear in your community, it's the inside of you that feels void and trivial.

When you're out there dropping money, that huge emotional hole within you feels almost filled and--if only for a bit --you feel great.

Heavy-duty self-denial is a major element of addictive behavior. In order to ascertain whether or not you're enduring spending addiction, you're going to have to do a unsparingly truthful "inspection" of your spending habits: how much and how frequently you spend; what harm your spending has on your bank account, your employment, your loved ones, and your very personal life; and, first and foremost, what feelings of dread and/or insecurity your spending habits try to cover.

Realizing you might have an addiction is the beginning big step toward recovery. If you surmise that spending is a probable source of troubles for you, you may consider speaking with a therapist.

Together you are able to view what motivates you to purchase things and how your spending habits impact the gist of your life, which is to say, how it forms the way you relate to those near to you, how you imagine you're viewed by other people, and how you truly feel about yourself.

Addictive conduct is treatable. If you really wish to put a stop to how your spending habits are absorbing your life, therapy may provide insight that will help you un-learn counter-productive conduct, and guide the way to acquiring fresh coping skills that will let you claim the "invaluable" gift of true happiness and self-contentment.

The signals and symptoms of compulsive spending addiction or shopping addiction are really like to other addictions such as sexual addiction, Net addiction, and food addiction.

Demeanors distinctive of compulsive shopping and spending include the accompanying:

• Shopping as a result of feeling downhearted, defeated, dejected, angry or frightened

• Shopping or spending habits inducing emotional distress in one's living

• Getting into arguments with other people about one's shopping or disbursal habits

• Experiencing a sense of loss without charge cards

• Experiencing an on edge feeling, disturbed, or cranky when you have not been able to purchase something

• Spending more than you are able to afford

• Purchasing items on credit that wouldn't be purchased with hard cash

• Experiencing a rush of euphoria and anxiousness when spending money

• Experiencing guilt, feeling ashamed, embarrassed or discombobulated after shopping or spending money

- Lying to other people about purchases made or how much revenue was spent

- Thinking overly about money

- Spending a lot of time juggling accounts or bills to oblige spending

Compulsive shopping or spending might result in interpersonal, occupational, family and financial troubles in one's life story. In a lot of ways the results of this behavior are similar to that of whatever other addiction.

Damage in relationships might occur as a consequence of excessive spending and attempts to cover up debt or purchases. Individuals who engage in compulsive shopping or spending might become obsessed with that conduct and spend less and less time with crucial individuals in their lives.

They might experience anxiousness or depression as a result of the spending or shopping which might interfere with employment or school functioning.

Financial troubles might come about if money is borrowed or there's unreasonable utilization of credit to make purchases. Frequently the extent of the financial harm is distinguished only after the shopper or spender has amassed a big debt that necessitates a drastic alteration in life-style to resolve.

What causes it?

- Emotional lack in childhood

- Incapability to tolerate negative feelings

- Need to fill an interior void

- Thrill seeking

- Approval seeking

- Perfectionism

- Genuinely impulsive and compulsive

- Need to be in control

Shopping and Trauma

There are as a lot of reasons to overshop as there are over shoppers. Every one is a way of trying to deal with barbed individual problems and unmet personal wants. Mostly individuals shop to comfort themselves, temporarily ease depression, defeat negative self image, or to prevent dealing with something else. For a few individuals, compulsive shopping is a reaction to stress, lose, or trauma, and an attempt to feel more in control.

Occasionally individuals utilize compulsive shopping as a weapon, to express angriness or seek revenge. Or, a few might shop to hang on to love, as in the compulsive gift giver. In the final analysis, compulsive purchasing is an attempt to settle a personal issue or spiritual quandary.

Heal

Distinguishing the Trauma.

In order to comprehend, defeat and prevent these hurts, we must recognize what they are and what we may do to finally break the cycle from carrying on in our own family. For instance, picking up on our parents' personality traits may be one of these. If you've a parent that's hot-tempered and raised their voice a great deal, this is one thing that may be prevented.

When you are able to identify the trauma and reach the core of it, you'll be able to keep it from cycling through your own family.

Forgiving Other People.

To be able to march on after any trauma (at any time) is to forgive the individual who induced it. If you were ill-treated as a youngster in any way, this might be a really hard step for you. It's even difficult as a grownup. It's difficult, yet really crucial.

Emotional Mending.

Individuals have different means of dealing with matters, emotionally. There might be times where you'll feel the anguish from trauma, as a similar occasion sneaks up. Perhaps something occurred that reminded you of that harm. How will you defeat those negative emotions? You might find it in prayer or another form. Coming through trauma, emotionally is a chore, but may be done.

Mental Welfare.

When you're traumatized mentally, it impacts your whole being, from emotional to physical facets. There are things that you are able to do to get yourself back into your correct mind. Naturally there are medicines to cover up the root of the issue. Then there are physicians to give it a name. All the same, in order to truly get over it, you must distinguish it and be strong enough to master it, when it comes back to you.

Faith.

This is a really big word when it bears on sufferers of trauma. Who do you have faith in and why? Being a trauma survivor, I'll say that it begins with you. When you understand how to distinguish a potential situation that may lead to trauma, understand how to deal with it when it attempts to come at you and in the end prevent it, this makes it easier to trust other people. Keeping your guard up is great, depending upon the circumstance. All the same, when you learn not to let individuals impact you, while maintaining an open mind, you'll discover that it becomes easier to trust other people on a certain level. Faith is obtained in levels and trauma survivors may relate to this. Time is a healer and faith is a must!

Relinquishing.

In order to trust other people and wholly, understand that relinquishing these past pains is something that you must do. You might never forget about them, but letting them go from impacting your life, is crucial for advancing, trusting and holding new relationships.

Marching On.

Not mastering your past pains, traumas and bombed relationships (whatever the instance) keeps you from marching on. Sure you might advance; all the same you'll be carrying these with you to impact your relationships. These may be relationships with your own youngsters or even your mate. It harms them, as you're hurting. There's nothing that they may do and it may finally ruin that relationship with them. The reason is because they're attempting to make you happy and happy. It's impossible for them to do this, as it's something you may only do for yourself.

Encountering, Knowing and Loving Yourself.

This is the greatest step of all. Once you've gone through the mending, trusting and relinquishing process, it's time to take your life back. This is a big step and it's like a new start. You know that you are able to love again, beginning with yourself and deal with your addictions. This is the most crucial step. Loving yourself looks like its miles away when you've been traumatized as a youngster. Youngsters look to grownups for all their needs. These include emotional needs. The last thing that they anticipate is to be hurt by any grownup. Ultimately loving yourself lets you really see the love that other people have for you.

Loving and assisting others.

This is a good step and helps to carry on your emotional mending. When you get to a place where you are able to assist others, it makes you feel great. It enables you to be free to love and it likewise assists you mentally, also.

Beyond the Diet with Healthy Diet Recipes

There's a lot of self gratitude in loving individuals and you are able to easily assist them, when you've gone through the same that they're experiencing.

Living a Good Life.

Now you're able to live and be glad. You are able to place trauma, address it, get over it and assist other people.

There's no keener feeling in the world then to be able to assist other people that you recognize you are able to help. You are able to enjoy your loved ones and assist them as well. You'll recognize what not to do, forbidding the cycle of harm in your own family. You'll feel triumphant in knowing that you've overcome and now you are able to love and know you're loved.

Being free from childhood injury seems like it's a million miles away to somebody who's affected and can't break the cycle. It may be done, even if it takes a long time.

CHAPTER 6- BINGE SPENDING: SOCIETY DICTATES

We approval seekers are individuals who will do anything to get affirmation and acceptance from other people.

Approval seekers like me tend to believe that we're being great (saintly! angelic!) when we let other people have their way with us in exchange for a hit of praise. The individuals in our lives are likely to reward our sickness, as we'll do pretty much anything to please them, and what's not to enjoy about that?

Here's what: Being dependent upon approval—so dependent that we trade away all our time, energy, and personal finances to get it—wrecks lives.

Approve Of Yourself

In our world of blended cultures and customs, we might face countless moral codes, all different from each other. There's simply no way to earn approval from each of these disparate origins; attempting to do so will make you feel even more insecure. Rather, clearly specify your own moral code and then stick with it whether or not other people approve.

Right now consider something you plan to do in the coming days that you don't wish to do: host a boring guest, send greeting cards to people you scarcely know, overspend to the point of severe financial strain. Then make believe that your best friend, instead of you, is the one pondering this action. What would you say is her ethical obligation? Don't think manners; think ethical code. Would it be sincerely unethical for your friend to invite only people she likes, or send out no greeting cards, or purchase fewer presents?

Take a little time working out your true beliefs.

If you resolve your objectionable plans aren't ethical requirements, but you do them anyhow, you're selling out. Anything we do entirely to please other people, in the absence of either true desire or ethical necessity is a way of selling ourselves, our lives, and our power.

Ask yourself whether the dosage of approval you look to gain from this behavior is worth losing a piece of the true you. I would be the last one to label you if the answer is yes. All I expect is that you be cognizant that this is selling out, not virtuousness.

Among the most beneficial ways to break your dependency on approval is to arrange up a situation in which the sole way to acquire approval is to get disapproval. To utilize this technique, call an acquaintance, tell her you're going out to acquire some disapproval, and ask her to shower you with praise later. It works even more if you have several individuals—your best chums, your therapy group, your stitching circle—waiting to hear the narrative of your uprising.

The brilliance of the strategy is that whether or not you carry through with your intents, somebody is going to disapprove. Finding out how to deal with that may prevent a lifetime of selling out.

Are you committed to saying yes to each request? Are you fatigued from accepting every invitation to help other people in one way or another? Do you find yourself finishing tasks for other people before attending to your responsibilities?

I've often found myself in YES domain. In Yes domain the sole answer that matters pleases somebody else. How do you say no to colleagues, loved ones, and friends when you're overwhelmed? It's not simple to say no, but it's essential in order to maintain healthy limits.

Arrive at a list of reasons why you feel they want to please other people. How do you feel when you agree to a request that causes you to overextend yourself? If you're perpetually displaying this type of conduct, tension, anxiety, stress, and physical exhaustion are inevitable.

Make healthy limits. Individuals will persist in taking as long as you give. It's crucial to understand when you reach your limit. If you don't make boundaries and convey your expectations effectively, you'll continue to feel overpowered.

Accept yourself. Why are you saying yes to so many requests? Are you looking for approval from other people? Is your need for approval linked to prior events in your life? Be truthful with yourself, quit seeking approval, and recognize that true love isn't contingent on your reaction to please others.

Don't regret your reaction. What good are you to yourself if you spend all of your time pleasing other people? The individuals in your life will learn to live with a no from you, or they'll ask somebody else. You must walk in truth, and walking in truth entails giving an honest reaction to a request!

Shopping isn't simply a woman's thing. Studies demonstrate that men and women were nearly equally likely to be compulsive buyers. They do shop differently, though. Men tend to shop more in a "work" form and women are more "leisure time" shoppers. Women--who tend to be other-oriented and relationship-centered--tend to purchase apparel, jewelry, cosmetics, and appearance orientated goods. While men--who tend to be self-oriented and activity-centered--often buy electronics and sporting goods, chiefly functional goods. Men and women likewise relate differently to what they have...women treasure their emotional and symbolic possessions, while men prefer their functional and leisure items.

Likewise, men's shopping is more culturally accepted. We tend to see men more as consumers and collectors, but not shoppers. While a woman's buying habits are frequently seen as self-indulgent and insignificant. Call it what you will, the fact is that both genders are subject to severe abuses when it comes to purchasing behavior.

Ways To Curb Buying

Be a private detective around your purchasing behavior. Distinguish the cues or triggers that lead to over shopping or overspending, e.g. a foul day at work, a battle with a mate, feeling lonesome, blasé, or in need of pay back, spare time, or the holidays maybe.

Seek patterns and associations. It's crucial to recognize that shopping is an equal opportunity, general-purpose mood changer, but works only temporarily. After a brief while, your mood will frequently dip even below where it was previously as now the shame and the remorse are imparted to it.

View the outcomes of your over shopping. In what regions of your life is it costing you? Financially? Emotionally? Socially? Occupationally? Spiritually?

Pick out somebody in your life to be a buying back up chum and brainstorm together about how that individual will support you to quit over shopping.

Anticipate that you might very likely feel sorrier before you feel better, since the anesthetic qualities that the purchasing supplied are now gone.

Put down everything you spend and allot each expenditure a score, based on how essential you deem it to be, from 0=totally unneeded, to 1/3=a bit essential, to 2/3=really essential to 1, crucial. At the close of the week, view how many of your buys you rated totally or relatively unneeded and then you'll see how much you may save if you were only purchasing things that were more essential instead of less.

Make certain you apportion a little money monthly for things that make your heart whistle. Otherwise, you're placing yourself at risk for feelings of deprivation and a spending splurge.

Confer with one of the many net calculators that will help you to discover the high cost of charge card debt.

Take charge of your prompts by avoiding them altogether, or limiting your vulnerability. If Wal-Mart is a prompt...

Remain far away!

Likewise build in a break between your impulse to purchase and your real purchasing behavior. During the break, ask yourself:

- How come I'm here?

- How do I feel?

- Do I have to have this?

- What if I hold off?

- How will I pay for this?

- Where will I place it?

Use cash or a debit card, without overdraft protection. Know what's in your checking account at all times.

Attain a list of your most beneficial reasons to quit over shopping. Retain this "Stop Shopping?" list with you at all times.

Question yourself: What Am I Truly Shopping For? What rudimentary emotional needs have tripped my urge to overshop? Rather than shopping, do something else that's good for you and life-enhancing to meet some of your rudimentary needs. If you shop because you're lonesome, find a different way to feel associated that builds self-regard, not tears it down!

Remember: you are able to never acquire enough of what you don't truly need.

CHAPTER 7- BINGE SPENDING: ASSESS YOUR FINANCIAL STATUS

• What major fiscal challenges do you face?

• State your financial positives in terms of revenue, debt management, and savings.

• How do you think you arrived at this point—and what would you like to see altered?

• How well organized are you for a financial emergency? Write it out now: The amount we have put away an emergency fund is   .

• How is the subject of money addressed in your family: emotionally or rationally?

• Who makes the fiscal decisions? How come? How much collaboration is there?

Why it counts: Clarity and commitment. Authorities agree that before crunching the numbers, families needs to scrutinize their financial wellness—and the best chance of success comes from having both mates on board.

Here we will explain to you the basic principle of personal financial ratio and its analyses. This will help you keep a tab on your personal finances.

Now what are personal finance ratios, you'd ask.

As the name hints these ratios deal with your personal riches, assets or cash in hand. All the more they're exceedingly simple to understand. Just plain discipline of sustaining a budget and statement of assets (what you earn or have) and liabilities (what you spend or what you owe to other people) will help you check your financial wellness.

Here is an easy guide which will help you to comprehend these ratios in detail. Let us have a look as to how these ratios may help.

Basic solvency ratio

This ratio signals your power to meet monthly expenses in case of any emergency or calamity. It's calculated by dividing the near-term cash you have with your monthly expenses.

Basic solvency ratio = Cash / Monthly expenses (this ratio isn't mentioned in percentage).You are able to also call it as emergency or contingency preparation ratio. This ratio helps you prepare for unexpected troubles.

Beyond the Diet with Healthy Diet Recipes

An illustration, a 30-year-old businessman whose wife had an emergency gall bladder surgery last year. In spite of the fact that they had enough insurance to take care of exactly such an event, due to a few administrative problems on the day of discharge, he was informed that he would have to pay in cash as the bill couldn't be settled.

He had a hard time arranging the funds on an emergency fundament. He was fortunate to have good acquaintances and relatives who lent him the money. But not everyone have such great admirers or relatives to bail them out at such short notice. I'm sure no one wants to be in the same shoes.

Therefore we have to be organized for such a situation. How? By sustaining an emergency fund!

Let's examine how much money is adequate. Here is where basic solvency ratio comes handy.

The numerator of the basic solvency ratio formula, cash (near cash), would commonly comprise of the following things:

• Savings account

• Bank fixed deposits

• Liquid funds

• Cash on hand

The above elements are liquid assets which come on hand at the first possible hint of financial problems. Liquid funds may be delivered immediately. Same goes for fixed deposits as they may be broken and liquidated at once in case of an emergency.

Monthly expenses:

Only the mandatory fixed and varying expenses are taken here for ease. Any amusement outlay shouldn't be taken as these expenses can be quashed.

Mandatory fixed expenses include the income you pay for, loans, insurance premium, and rent.

Mandatory varying expenses, on the other hand, comprise of food, transit, clothing/ personal care, medical care, utilities, education expenses and assorted compulsory expenses (the above expenses can vary depending upon individuals).

The total of the above divided by 12 (that is 12 months) helps you attain the monthly average as your variable expenditure might change. Assuming that you've cash of 60,000 and median monthly expenses of 25,000 your basic solvency ratio would work out to: 60,000 / 25,000 = 2.4.

But is it great?

Not quite. An Ideal ratio should come to 3. What does the number 3 mean?

It means that you must have money equal to or at least 3 months of your mandatory expenses in a contingence or emergency fund.

How come just 3 months? This is because research shows that 3 months time is enough to emerge from any type of financial pinch. As individuals near their retirement age, they should make certain that this fund is kept up to six months of their required expenses. The fund should be divided and kept in the form of cash, fixed deposit, or liquid fund.

CHAPTER 8- BINGE SPENDING: FINANCIAL PRIORITIES

It's so crucial to set your financial priorities in life as this may help secure your financial future. Too much stress could come from mishandled funds. Some individuals might make mistakes in setting their financial priorities like saving more for their children's college education and a lesser for their own retirement.

Set Goals

You should understand how to prioritize your financial goals so that you'll stay pleased and financially stable as you get older in life. This doesn't mean that you don't consider the future of your kids but you're just setting your financial priorities in order.

Set an amount monthly for food, water and shelter as these are your primary needs. You need to think about buying various healthy foods and attempt to avoid unneeded snacks that are unhealthy. You likewise need to do your best in your present job as it's your source of income to pay for your utility bills, home mortgage or rent, and groceries. This is where you start setting your priorities straight.

A few individuals are so frugal on their grocery shopping, they disregard their health needs just to buy expensive gadgets or airplane tickets for a leisure time. Observe that attending to your own daily needs is your duty and priority to prevent evading the rent or house mortgage, utilities and other crucial matters for well-being particularly if you have a family.

Occasionally this could be the cause of disagreement between man and wife for they've different views when it comes to income management. The other mate wants to spend most of the money and isn't afraid of financial debt while the other one prefers to save something for the rainy days or an emergency. Be a good role model to your youngsters as they think highly of you as a parent.

Pay your charge card debt if you have any. Paying-off the charge card with the highest rate of interest then followed by the ones with lower rates of interest is the best thing that you can do in order to eradicate your entire charge card debt. Purchase things or goods with cash as much as possible and contain your spending habits.

Prevent over using your charge card so that you'll be able to continue to have access to your accounts if you truly need it. Some individuals, who were working and never bothered to save for an emergency fund and over used their credit, now have nothing. You don't want to be in a spot where you've no earnings and can't even access your credit cards because your accounts are closed.

Center on saving enough cash for your emergency fund particularly when all of your credit card debt is paid-off. This is really crucial in case of a job loss or other major unforeseen things that might happen to you or anybody in your family. Avoid the enticement of purchasing things that you are able to just live without and center on building your emergency savings.

Setting your financial priorities should be your principal ambition. Have a clear list of the crucial things that will cover your monthly expenses and finances and number each item from the highest to the lowest with regards to their importance and need.

Step-up your 401(k) or a 403(b) contribution and retirement savings if you already have enough cash savings for your emergency fund. Try to save 15%-20% of your salary for retirement.

Try to save for your retirement before saving for your youngsters' college education. When your youngsters grow up, they can use student loans, get scholarships or attend a good community college or state university where it's more affordable. As you consider their future, you likewise need to think of your golden years.

Capitalize on free training opportunities. Attending free seminars and trainings to advance your knowledge is a very good investment for your future. Setting career goals in life is really crucial as the job market is highly competitive.

Revise or update your will to make certain that your wishes are secure and accomplished. You need to have estate planning regardless how small your estate is. Some individuals will just assume that their assets and possessions will automatically pass to their family but without a legal will, the State might step-in and allocate your property or estate.

Valuate your insurance coverage. Check whether your car and homeowner policies are updated and their deductibles are fair. You might seek life insurance particularly if you're the head of the family working full-time. You may likewise think about buying long-term-care insurance, to aid you in paying for nursing care or assisted-living when you get old.

Stick To it

In today's domain there are very few individuals who take the time to produce a personal budget. Some individuals don't see the value in doing so; others merely have no desire to confine their spending habits. With this in mind, it should surprise no one that the number of personal bankruptcies has achieved an all time high. Individuals have achieved a point in our society where they purchase on impulse with no thoughts to the outcomes. In order to reverse these trend individuals need to become more responsible with their forms of spending. Among the best tools to help a person achieve this conduct is the personal budget.

A personal budget is a financial plan which sets bounds on the sum of money that will be spent on each category of expenses in a given month. A beneficial budget will take into consideration such elements as: the amount of income being obtained, owed debt to be retired, retirement savings, and an emergency fund.

A lot of individuals have no idea precisely where or how they spend a good portion of their income. How many times have you taken money from the ATM only to realize a few days later that it's gone? Many times it's hard to remember how precisely you spent the money, and frequently this money is wasted on frivolous buys. A budget will help avoid this by making an individual accountable for the income that they spend. If an individual only has $50 left for monthly food expenses then they might decide to give up purchasing that fancy $3 designer cup of coffee.

A different benefit is that a budget depicts an accurate idea of how much a person can actually afford to pay for assorted consumer items. Whether it's a home, a car, or a new TV set, an individual will be able to ascertain whether or not a particular purchase will fit within their monetary constraints. This acts as a precaution against getting in over your head financially.

It's crucial to realize that merely creating a budget isn't enough. This in and of itself will do an individual absolutely no good if he doesn't discipline himself to stick to it. Occasionally this will very hard, especially if an individual has founded the habit of freely spending without an afterthought. However, the long-run advantages of financial freedom, debt free living, and a comfortable retirement far outbalance any potential difficulty.

Be Proactive

List as many of these bills as you are able to identify over a 12-month period.

Now, employ the "one-twelfth" rule, where you put aside funds for these expenses monthly, so as to limit their impact when payments come due.

Next, center on where you are able to spend less money without depriving yourself.

• What uneconomical or indulgent practices can you cut down on? (Cab rides when you are able to walk, expensive lunches.)

• Do you shop for items you don't require?

• Are you paying too much for services like car insurance, cable or cell phone service?

• Do you have unused memberships (e.g. gym) that you're still paying for (and may sell)?

It's easy to distinguish between the two if you go by a textbook definition. But actually, the distinction is hard and has been getting narrower over the past few years.

Nowadays, a car has become an emotional need in spite of the existence of an efficient public transport system. The need for an auto has transformed from a status symbol to a luxury to a basic essential now. The same system of logic applies to food. From home food to a fast food joint, nowadays buyers expect a fine dining experience and not just good food. This ambience comes at a premium and individuals just don't mind paying for it.

The truth is, wants are inexhaustible and often the lines between needs and wants get blurred. Therefore, one needs to get into self-examination before giving into the impulse to splurge.

Let's presume a family of 4 spends $8,000 on food, $25,000 on shelter, $20,000 on education and $10,000 on transportation. Now calculate the difference between your outlay and earnings. All you have to do is to write the primary price list and the cost of living in your city and compare the areas to give you a truthful picture.

If you require a mobile because you've a field job, it's a need. But if you insist on the latest gadget which you are able to truly afford, it's a want. That was an easy pick. But it gets hard if you have to trade off an automatic washer for a refrigerator or substitute a radio with a home theatre-com-music system. .. Think about it!

Chapter 9- Binge Spending vs. Habitual Saving

Among the oldest rules of personal finance is the easy word of advice to pay yourself first. All the money books tell you to do it. All the personal finance blogs say it, too. Even your parents have given you the same advice.

But it's difficult. That money could be used somewhere else. You could pay the telephone bill, could pay down debt, and could buy a new videodisc player. You've tried once or twice in the past, but it's so simple to forget. You don't keep a budget, so when payday comes around; the income just finds its way elsewhere.

To pay yourself first means merely this: Before you pay your bills, before you buy foodstuffs, before you do anything else, allow a portion of your income for savings. Put the income into your 401(k), your Roth IRA, or your savings account. The first bill you pay monthly should be to yourself. This habit, acquired early, may help you build tremendous wealth.

Once you pay yourself first, you're mentally founding saving as a priority. You're telling yourself that you're more important than the light company or the landlord. Building savings is a potent motivator — it's empowering.

Paying yourself first furthers sound financial habits. Most individuals spend their money in the following order: bills, fun, saving.

Unsurprisingly, there's generally little left over to put in the bank. But if you bump saving to the front — saving, bills, fun — you're able to set the income aside before you justify reasons to spend it.

By paying yourself first, you're constructing a cash buffer with real life applications. Steady contributions are an excellent way to build a savings. You can use the money to deal with emergencies. You can utilize it to purchase a home. You can utilize it to save for retirement. Paying yourself first gives you freedom — it opens a domain of opportunity.

The best way to acquire a saving habit is to make the process as painless as conceivable. Make it automatic. Make it invisible. If you arrange to have the money taken from your paycheck before you get it, you'll never know it's gone.

The true barrier to acquiring this habit is discovering the money to save. Many individuals believe it's impossible. But almost everybody can save at least 1% of their income. That's only one penny out of every dollar. A few will argue that saving this little is non-meaningful. But if a skeptic will attempt to save just 1% of his money, he'll commonly discover the process is painless. Perhaps next he'll try to save 3%. Or 5%. As his saving rate increases, so his savings will grow.

If you're scrambling to find money to save, consider setting aside your next raise for the future. As your income grows, set your gains aside for retirement and savings. Once you're imparting the maximums to your retirement (and you've built emergency savings), you are able to start to utilize your raises for yourself again.

Pay yourself first, my friends. It's a habit that you'll never regret.

Dig Out

If you've run up a lot of charge card debt, begin paying off the one with the highest rate of interest first. Mathematically, this will save you the most interest. But, if you've several smaller charge card balances, then you might feel like you're making more progress by paying them off individually first.

Begin keeping really close track of your spending. A number of little comforts in your budget might have to be eliminated in order to make ends meet. Restaurants, cinemas and other expensive entertainment may be substituted with libraries, galleries and outdoor exercise.

Papers, magazine subscriptions and cable TV are likewise good candidates for budget cuts. One expenditure that might be worthwhile, however, is a personal finance program that trails your debts, assets and cash flow on a day by day basis, so that you recognize precisely where you stand at all times.

Whatever you do, do not miss a payment. Late payments may truly hurt your credit score, and thus make it even more grueling for you to secure more positive financing. This may affect your insurance rates likewise. Making the lower limit payment by the deadline on your credit card is much brighter than making a larger payment a couple of days late.

A second source of income may make a huge difference to debtors. If you are able to earn just $500 a month extra, that's $6,000 a year that you are able to apply toward debt reduction. Another thought is reducing the amount of tax you've withheld from your check. Having no tax deducted may be advantageous in some cases. Naturally, you'll have to pay the tax with interest and penalty at the end of the year, but these rates are typically much lower than standard charge card rates.

Don't hesitate to get help if you require it. Talk terms with creditors and see if you are able to work out a satisfactory settlement. Credit and financial counseling services may be invaluable resources and might be able to point you to options or tips that you'd never discover otherwise. They may likewise begin you on a debt management or consolidation program to help lower your rates.

Lastly, if all else fails, see if you are able to get a debt consolidation loan from a family member. You are able to offer to pay them a rate that's much lower than your charge card interest, but much higher than what they'd get in a checking or savings account.

Investments

Some steps to think about:

• Meet with a financial consultant or certified financial planner to view this all important part of your budgeting.

• Acquire a solid plan and stick with it. All too frequently we've become complacent when the market is doing well and cowardly when the market isn't doing so well. What sets the successful individuals apart is containing those emotions.

How come it matters: development—personally as well as financially. You've got to go from a spendthrift to budgeter, a budgeter to a saver, and a saver to an investor.

Ascertain what items or issues you're saving for. These may be retirement, a new house, your youngster's education or anything else you choose.

Ascertain when you want to retire, buy a house or send your youngsters to college, to help you decide what percentage return you need to earn on your initial investment.

Determine how much money to invest. Invest what you are able to comfortably afford now, keeping in mind that you are able to change that amount later.

Ascertain how much risk you're willing to take. Many investments bring forth high returns and are riskier than others.

When you decide the amount you're willing to invest, the returns you want to accomplish, when you need the money and how much risk you're willing to bear, assemble your investment portfolio.

An investment counselor or stockbroker is a great source of advice. Tell these advisers your objectives and ask them to propose how to allocate your income.

Reassess your portfolio at least yearly. Study each investment.

Change Some Things

Save income on electrical energy.

Put in the new type of fluorescent bulbs in lights you leave on for long periods. They provide 4 times as much light and last 10 times longer than incandescent bulbs. Likely Savings: $10-$50/yr.

Lower the temperature on your water heater to between 110 and 120 degrees. It's not essential to have it any hotter and wastes energy.

Likely Savings: $20-40/yr.

Discover if your utility company offers free energy audits, where they audit your home for energy effectiveness and advocate inexpensive ways to cut energy costs, like insulating the water heater, weather- stripping, and so forth. Just insulating your water heater may save you $25 a year. Likely Savings: $50/yr.

Set thermostats no greater than 68 degrees in winter and no lower than 78 degrees in summertime. Turn your heat down even more at night or when you're not home (unless you've a heat pump, which operates more efficiently at one uniform setting). Each extra degree in wintertime may increase heating costs by 3%. In summertime, each degree may raise cooling costs by 6%. Likely Savings: $325 to

$500/yr.

Cut down on the use of your dryer. Not only is it a huge energy drain, it may also suck heated air out of your home very quickly in wintertime. Hang clothes on a clothes rack to dry out and use the dryer for towels and other heavy items. Likely Savings: $25-50/yr.

Utilize your microwave rather than your oven if possible and save up to 50% in energy costs for cooking. Likely Savings: $50/yr.

Save income on water.

Always do full loads of wash. A typical full load utilizes about 21 gals of water. A little load uses 14 gals. Several small loads utilize substantially more water than one or two big loads. Over the course of a year, this adds up. Likely Savings: $25-$125/yr.

Run your dish washer only when you've a full load. Let the dishes air- dry rather than utilizing the heat cycle. An average dishwasher costs

$60 to $100 annually to run. Likely Savings: $35-55/yr.

Mend running toilets or leaking faucets quickly. An endlessly running toilet may utilize more than 8,000 gallons of water a year. Likely Savings: $25-125/yr.

Put in flow restricting shower heads. A family of 4 may save 8,000 to 12,000 gals of water a year. You not only save on the cost of the water, but likewise the cost of heating it. Likely Savings: $100-$300/yr.

Add fabric softener to your laundry at the suitable point in the cycle rather than adding it at the end and running a different rinse cycle, which may use up to ten extra gals of water. Figure out how much time it takes your washing machine to reach the rinse cycle, and set a timer so you are able to add softener at the right time. Likely Savings: $25-100/yr.

Utilize warm or cold water for washing apparel, and always rinse in cold water. Likely Savings: $50/yr.

Save money on other.

Use basic phone service. Extra services like call waiting and call forwarding may nearly double your costs for the phone. Likely Savings: $168/yr.

If you are able to live without cable, you are able to save between

$300 and $600 annually. If you can't live without it, acquire basic service only. You are able to rent a lot of movies for the extra $150 to $600 annually you pay for movie channels like HBO, Showtime, etc. Likely Savings: $144-700/yr.

Plant perennial flowers rather than annuals. You receive a onetime cost and enjoy the flowers for a long time, with little additional effort or income. Annuals, on the other hand, call for an outlay of cash and effort yearly. Likely Savings: $100-$300/yr.

Family Getaway and Not Binge Spending

Head out to the beach! Public beaches are free and amusing. You are able to also walk on the boardwalk. Have fun constructing sandcastles or sport fishing on the pier.

Go window browsing. Go to a strip mall and check up on the fresh arrivals. Just remember that you don't have to confine your window browsing to clothing stores. Stop by the window exhibits at electronics and jewelry stores. Fresh technical gadgets are always appearing on the market!

Ask about free company amenities. You might not know this, but a lot of times the company you work for has a list of places (i.e. museums and aquariums) that are free of charge if you give your work identification card at the admissions counter!

Beyond the Diet with Healthy Diet Recipes

View each season as a fresh way to have fun. In the summertime you are able to shoot hoops at the basketball court, play tennis or walk around the neighborhood with your acquaintances. In the autumn you are able to pull out your camera and take pictures of the fall leaves.

Fall is likewise a good time to go to a pumpkin patch. Wintertime is amusing because you are able to play in the snow or remain inside and watch the snow with a cup of hot chocolate or a café latte. Springtime is good for bicycling!

Ask in your friends for a night of board games, cards and charades. The cover charge is a little dish or drink of choice. Your donation will be the free entertainment, so be ready to host!

Stuck at home with the youngsters? Whether they're on vacation from school or visiting for the weekend, here's a couple of great suggestions on how to entertain them free of charge.

Think about going to free community festivals, free movie events and free parks.

Think about a day at the beach, a picnic in the park, hiking in the woods, or a different outdoor activity. Swimming, outdoor games and adventures are an affordable and effective way to spend the day with kids.

Have a rainy day list of thoughts ready likewise. Visit your local library and rent some kid-friendly films and play "movie theater": have the kids make up tickets, set up the front room like a movie theater and pop some popcorn. You are able to also make up your own board game with novelties around the house, produce drawing and coloring games, or do easy crafts.

Capitalize on ticket upgrades. It may cost a little more at the beginning, but consider year-round passes for local attractions for a good way to spend the day. Your local zoo or aquarium might offer such a deal, as well as funfairs and more.

Generally kids have capital ideas! Just be ready to give them a free or affordable option. For instance, if they suggest going out for ice cream, think about buying ice cream and cones at the food market instead and heading to the park. If they want to go out for pizza pie, purchase grocery items to make a pizza and turn it into an activity alternatively. A good imagination, and willingness to try fresh things, will help you go a long way, and help you stretch your dollar while entertaining youngsters at the same time.

CHAPTER 10- TIPS AND SUMMARY ON HOW TO DO AWAY BINGE SPENDING

There has been a lot of not so fun info provided here.... But just because you're living on a budget, don't think you won't be able to have fun any longer. Sure, there will be some cutting you'll have to do - namely the frills. And you'll have to spend some time to find low-cost ways to have a good time. Remember to your early days, or when you were first wed. Remember when income was tight? Remember to what you did then for entertainment to get some ideas. Surely, there are things you are able to do now that you did back then and have the same kind of fun you had in those days.

Living a frugal life will give you a wide variety of benefits that you will extremely love. Being penny-wise will greatly help you to spend your money wisely and at the same time living within your means. It is very important that you have a clear and better understanding about the amazing benefits that you will encounter in living a frugal life.

• More Control

Living frugally will allow you to know the proper way to control spending your money. In this way, you will also determine where your funds go every single month.

• Better confidence

You will gain full confidence when you fully understand on how to control your finances. Living frugal life will also help you to boost your confidence level and making your own decisions that will have a great impact on your personal finances.

• Healthier Habits

Living frugally will prevent the occurrence of bad habits. In this way, you can be sure that you will obtain a healthy lifestyle that you dreamed of. Instead of buying unhealthy snacks, you can purchase on sale fruits that will suit with your budget.

• Less Stress

Living a frugal life will provide you with more freedom. You will also experience less stress since you are living within your means. An economical life will greatly help you to easily attain your long term goal and achieve your financial dreams in no time.

If you or a loved one have an issue with overspending or shopping (including a shopping addiction), it's sometimes crucial to seek professional help. Getting a psychological evaluation is a goodness opening move.

To address shopping addiction, therapists use cognitive- behavioral therapy to help the individual realize and change their behaviors. A few compulsive shoppers might learn to limit their shopping and for the most severe people a therapist might be in order.

It's not strange for addicts, as a whole, to have coexistent psychiatric disorders, like depression. Antidepressant medication might be considered as a treatment.

There are likewise 12-step programs for support, like Debtors Anonymous. And a lot of compulsive spenders chalk up of tens of thousands of dollars in bills, so credit counseling is likewise helpful.

Here is a review of a few basic changes in conduct that will have a big affect on breaking a shopping addiction:

• Accept that you're a compulsive spender, which is one- half the battle

- Do away with checkbooks and charge cards, which fuel the issue

- Don't shop by yourself as most compulsive shoppers shop solo and if you're with somebody you're much less likely to be spend

- Discover other meaningful ways to pass time

- Cut back temptations

- Make lists prior to going to the store; purchase what you require only – call people, take a trusted acquaintance

Anna Reed

- Wait so many hours prior to purchase

- Do you require this or do you merely want it?

- Formulate other ways to address emotions

- Formulate amusing things to do

And bear in mind that while behavior change is distinctly essential to recovery from compulsive spending, so is reaching out for assistance.

About The Author

Stephen Harris is a simple man with a big dream. He came from a simple family in Alabama but since Stephen has a big vision, he was able to build a business of his own.

Stephen wants to share his success and inspire others that are why he is now a financial consultant. He gets to talk to different schools as well on how to better manage finances at such a young age and let them understand how to properly build a credit score.